THE LITTLE BOOK OF BIG FASHION DATA

EDITION IV
2023

an analysis of 2023 high-fashion runway collections using data analytics software coded in python, to determine what's (objectively) in style

PARA ABUELO
the first engineer in the family

HOW TO READ THE DATA

all percentages correspond to the percentage of looks, or outfits, which exhibited each trend on a brand's runway

the looks seen on runways are not necessarily representative of what ends up in stores a couple of months later, but rather which trends designers are pushing out to the world and in which quantities

ALEXANDER McQUEEN

designed by Sarah Burton

SO MUCH MONOCHROME

monochrome

45%

nearly half of McQueen's 2023 runway looks were monochromatic, with a -35% decrease in the trend from the Spring to Fall collection

THE ACCENTS

26%

24%

cutouts

big sleeves

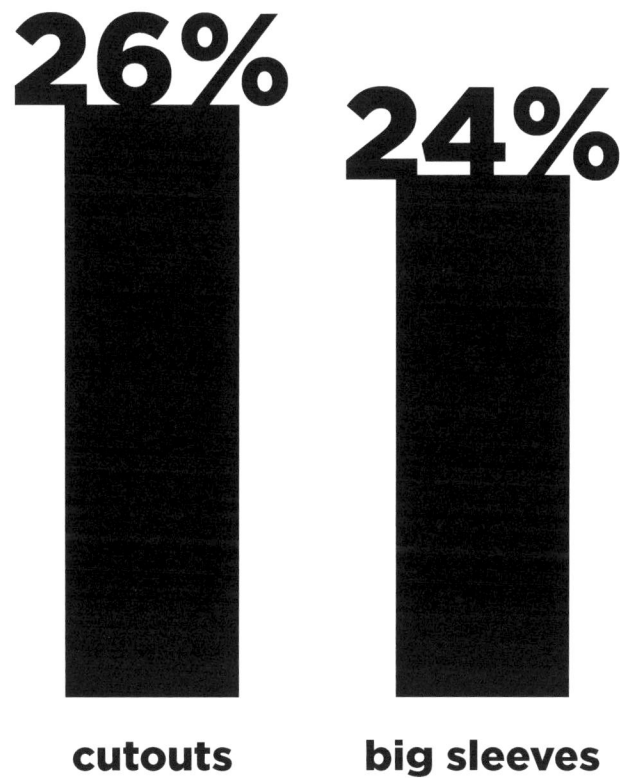

Alexander McQueen is never one to shy away from the unique or dramatic — from dresses and blazers in its Spring collection seemingly cut up with scissors, to 3-dimensional shoulder and sleeve accents in the Fall

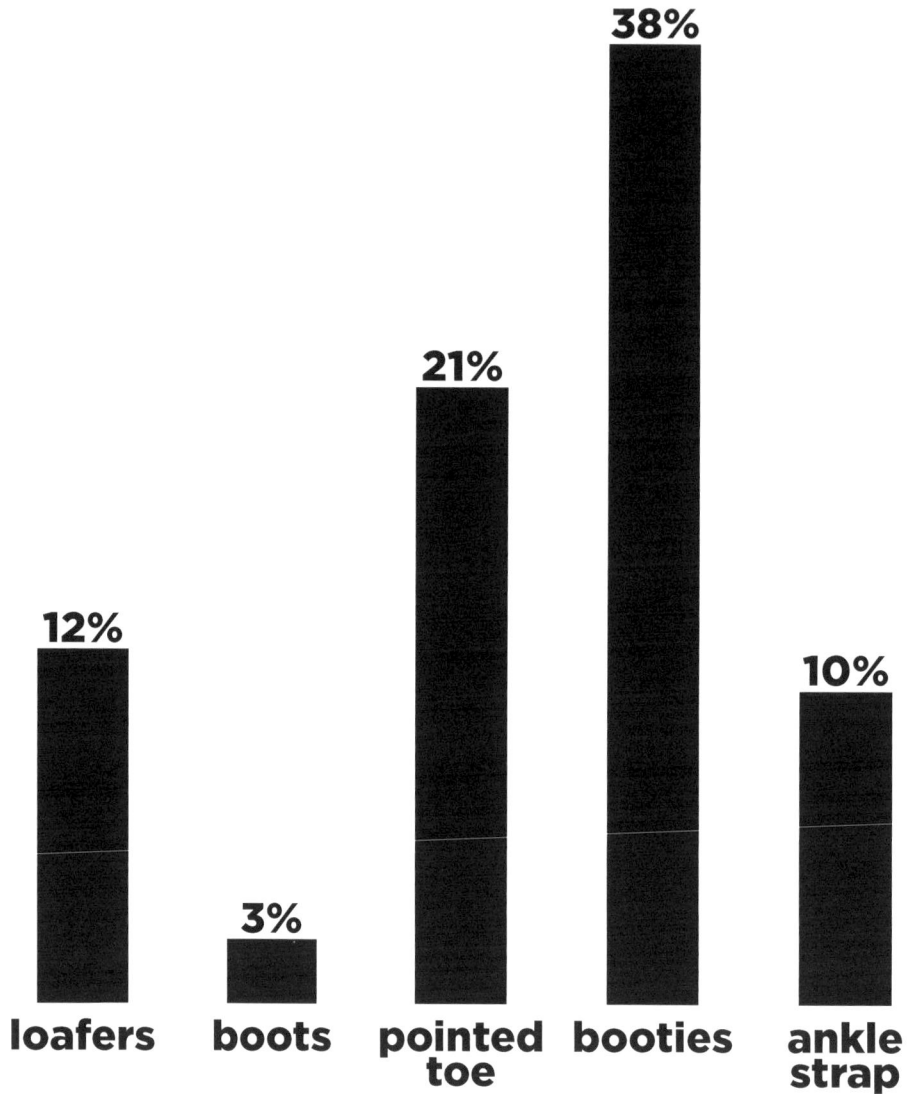

38%

21%

12%

10%

3%

loafers   boots   pointed   booties   ankle
                     toe   strap

ALL THE SHOES

from pointed-toe pumps to high leather
boots, Alexander McQueen included a variety of shoe options in his 2023 collections

tulle

tights

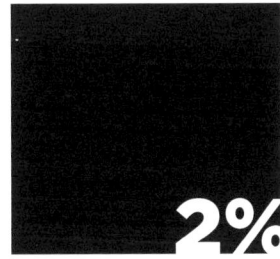

peplum

THE MICRO TRENDS*

*trends which were seen in less than 5% of
Alexander McQueen's runways this year

LOOK 23
SPRING / SUMMER 2023 RUNWAY

+37%
more dresses

spring
collection

fall
collection

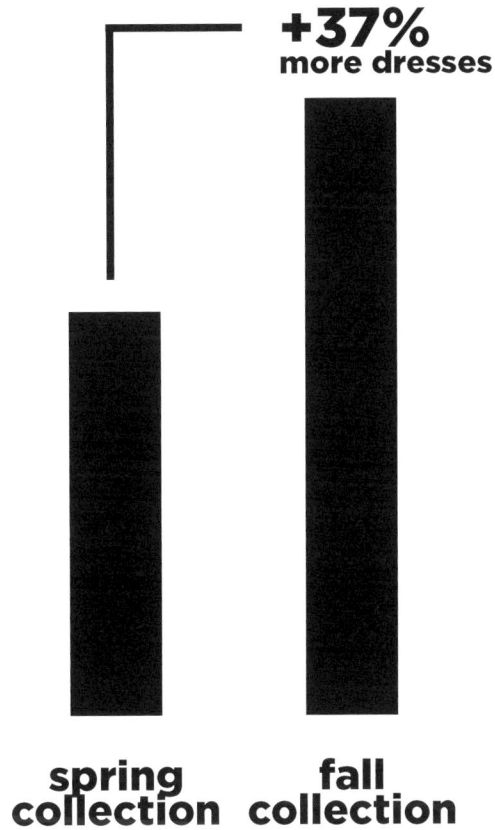

DRESSES FOR FALL

McQueen says dresses — from one-shoul-
dered leather pieces to shimmering, maxi-
length gowns — are more of a Fall staple

**mini
5%**

**high-low
20%**

**maxi
20%**

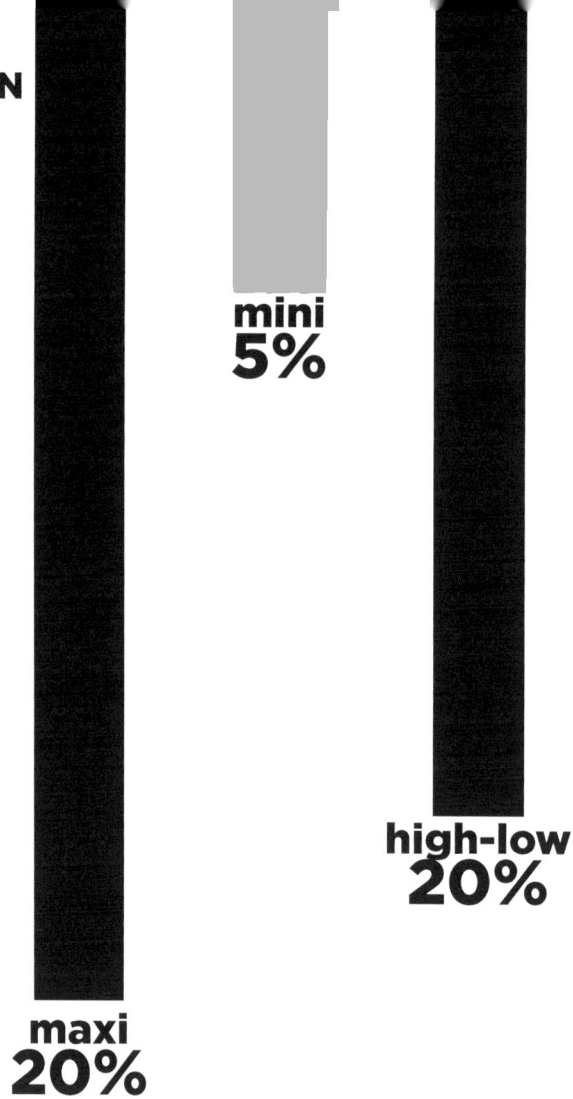

THE (LONG) HEMLINES

McQueen opted for longer hemlines this
year while prominently including "high-low"
gowns: mini-length in the front and maxi-
length in the back

HOW TO ACCESSORIZE

from leather shoulder bags to tight, waist belts, to colorful gloves, McQueen knows how to accessorize

7% gloves

14% shoulder bag

6% belts

BALMAIN

designed by Olivier Rousteing

BALMAIN

13% blazer

7% long coat

THE OUTERWEAR

Balmain says impeccably-tailored blazers
are the outerwear of choice this year

SHOES SHOES SHOES

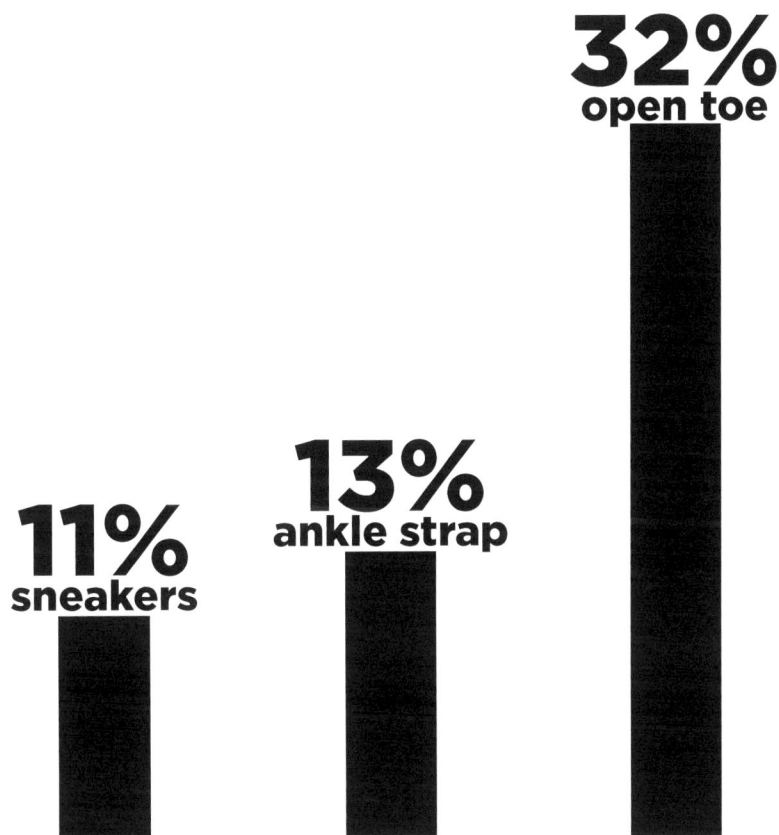

32%
open toe

13%
ankle strap

11%
sneakers

from oversized sneakers and large, padded ankle straps in Balmain's Spring collection to simple, patent leather flats and heels in the Fall, Balmain shows us you can never have too many shoes

+140%
more mini hemlines

spring
collection

fall
collection

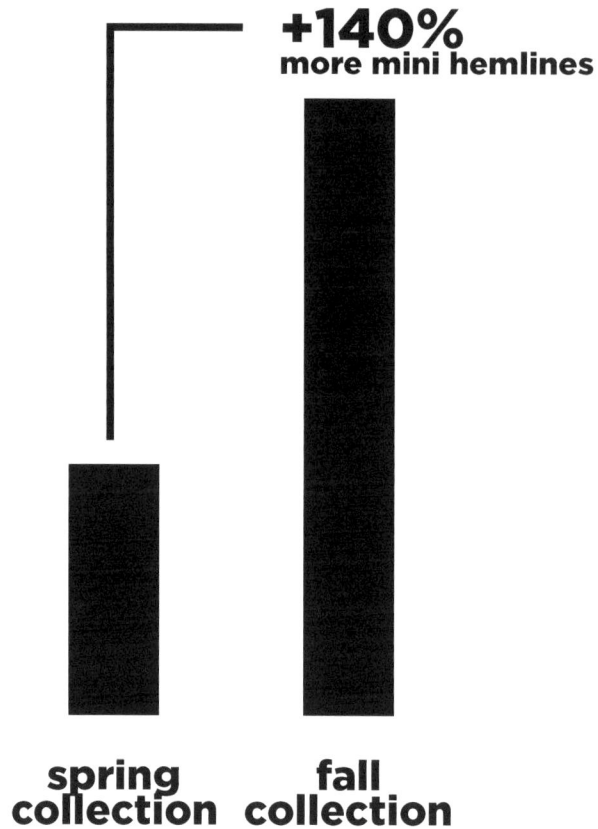

MINI SKIRTS?
FOR FALL?

mini-length hemlines — from short, tailored
dresses to leather mini skirts — were seen
increasingly more in Balmain's Fall collection than on the Spring runway

PANTS ARE ALWAYS IN

pants

45%

the most popular item analyzed across Balmain's collections was pants, seen in nearly
half of the Spring and Fall runways

THE BAGGAGE

Balmain showed versatile options for baggage this year, from woven leather and patterned shoulder bags, to shimmering clutch bags, to oversized totes

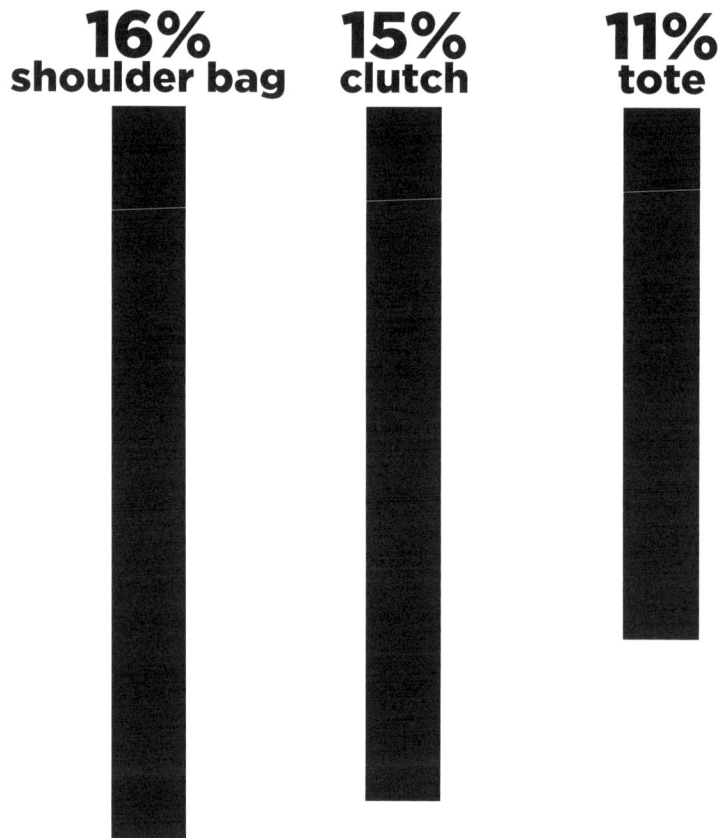

16%
shoulder bag

15%
clutch

11%
tote

LOOK 12
FALL / WINTER 2023 RUNWAY

45%
chunky jewelry

31%
hats

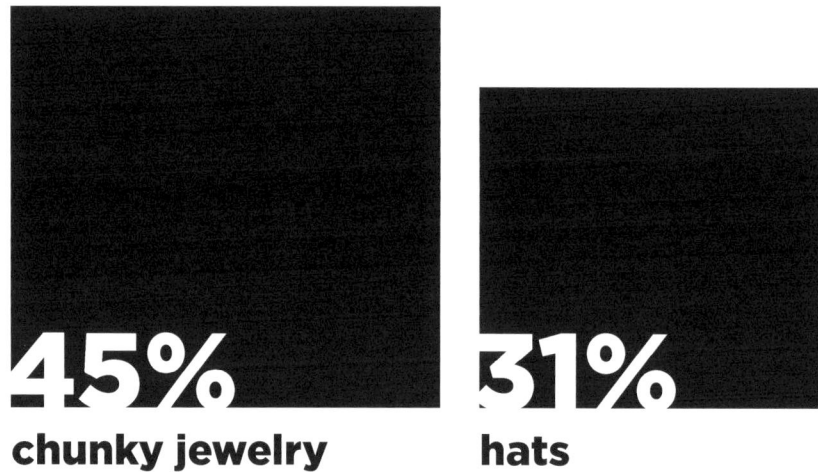

THE ACCESSORIES

the hats in Balmain's collections paid homage to founder Pierre Balmain, showing a refreshed design of his 1959 lampshade hat and 1970s berets

12%
woven

7%
shimmer

11%
sheer

5%
leather

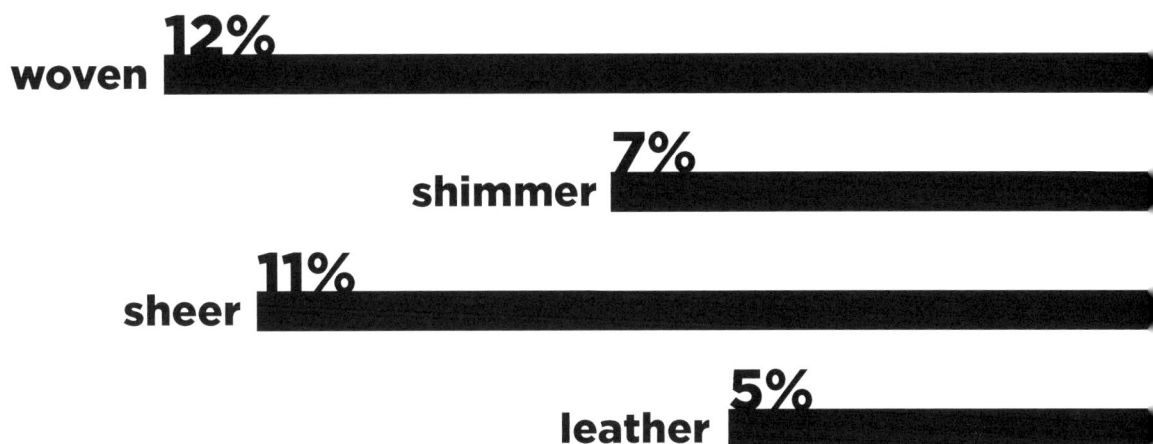

THE FABRICS & TEXTURES

Balmain did not shy away from experimenting with varying looks and feels this year — from sheer, printed dresses in the Spring collection to shimmering gowns in the Fall

BOTTEGA VENETA

designed by Matthieu Blazy

MIDI IS THE NEW MINI

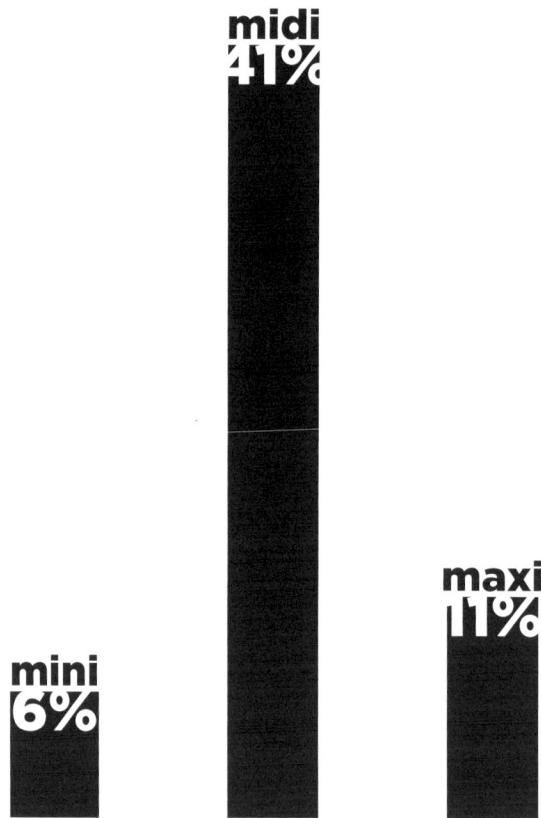

midi
41%

maxi
11%

mini
6%

the most common hemline used across
Bottega's collection this year was "midi":
clothing which falls below the knee but well
above the ankle

SUIT UP

button down, 21%

blazer, 14%

loafers, 13%

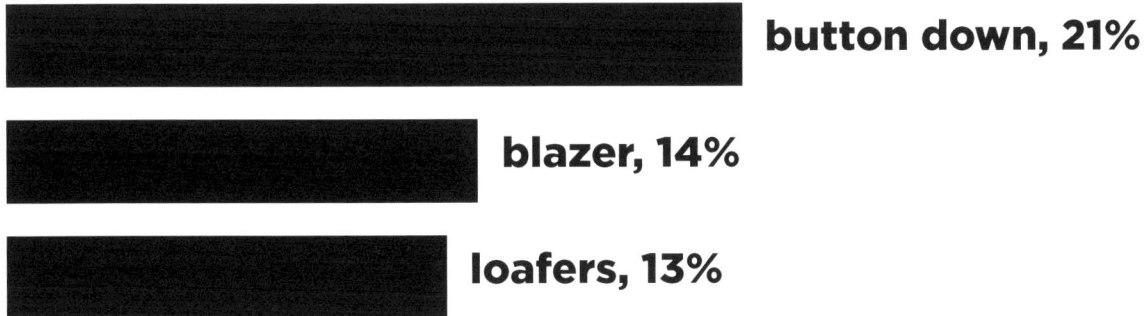

classic suiting staples — such as tailored blazers and layered button-down shirts — were seen prominently throughout Bottega's collections

THE FABRICS

Blazy introduced some interesting innovations with fabrics at Bottega — the opening looks of Bottega's Spring collection, while they *looked* like denim, flannel, and cotton, were actually all printed leather

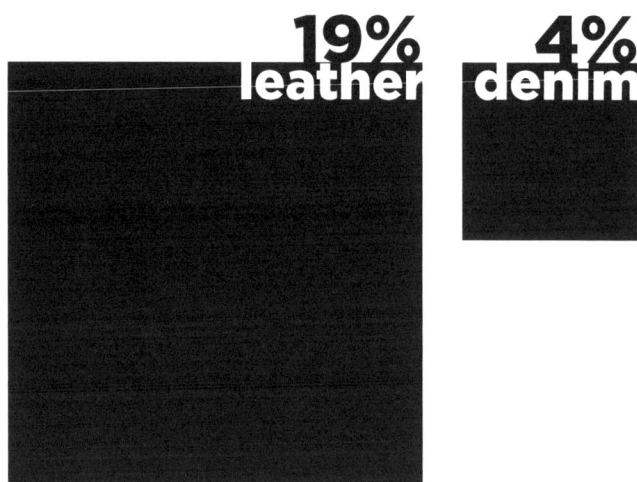

19%
leather

4%
denim

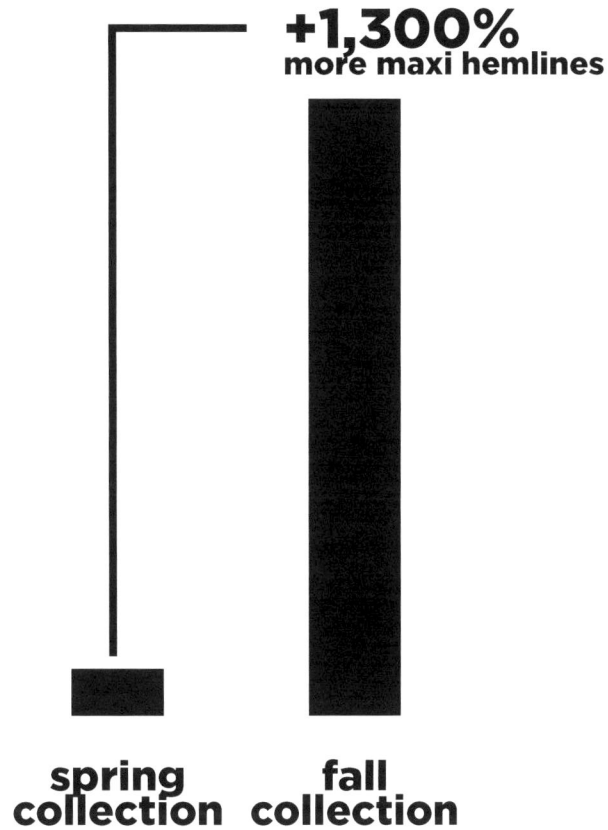

+1,300%
more maxi hemlines

spring
collection

fall
collection

MAXI-MALISM

Bottega's Fall collection included an over 1,300% increase in maxi-length hemlines compared to its Spring runway — seen across dresses, gowns, and long leather coats

LOOK 72
SPRING / SUMMER 2023 RUNWAY

SHOWING SOME SKIN

trends across Bottega Veneta's Spring and
Fall collections this year which exposed
some skin

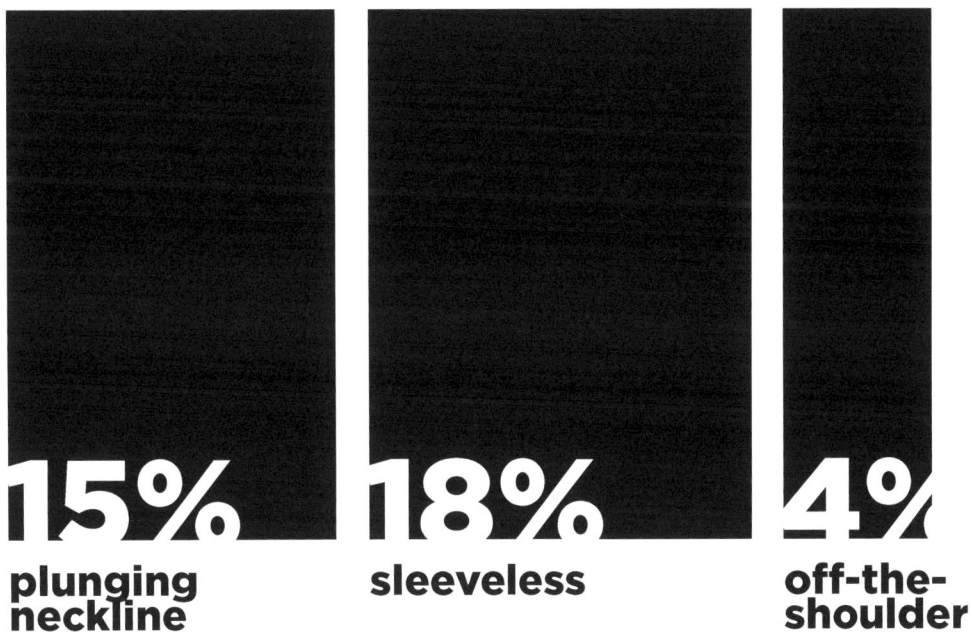

15%
**plunging
neckline**

18%
sleeveless

4%
**off-the-
shoulder**

lace
2%

tights
2%

stripes
3%

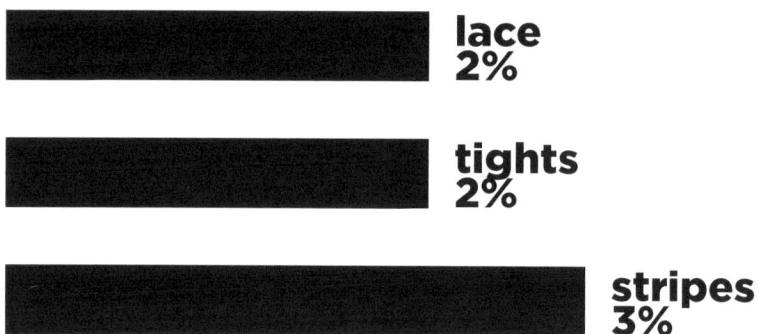

THE MICRO TRENDS*

*trends which were seen in less than 5% of
Bottega Veneta's runways this year

monochrome

35%

MORE MONOCHROME

over one third of Bottega's runway looks
this year were monochromatic, sticking to
just one simple color

BRANDON MAXWELL

designed by Brandon Maxwell

KEEPING IT SIMPLE

Brandon Maxwell's hallmark, high-fashion-yet-wearable looks leveraged some simple, wearable trends in this year's collections

t-shirt, 10%

denim, 3%

A COUPLE OF SHOE OPTIONS

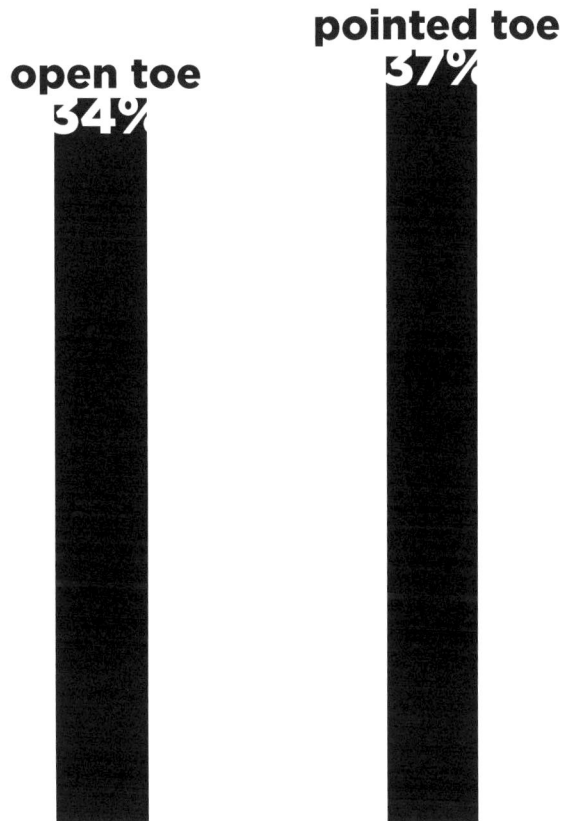

pointed toe
37%

open toe
34%

when it comes to shoes, Brandon Maxwell's most popular selections — pointed toe pumps and open-toed heels and sandals — showed up in similar proportions throughout his runways

3%
teddy fabric

3%
peplum

1%
cargo

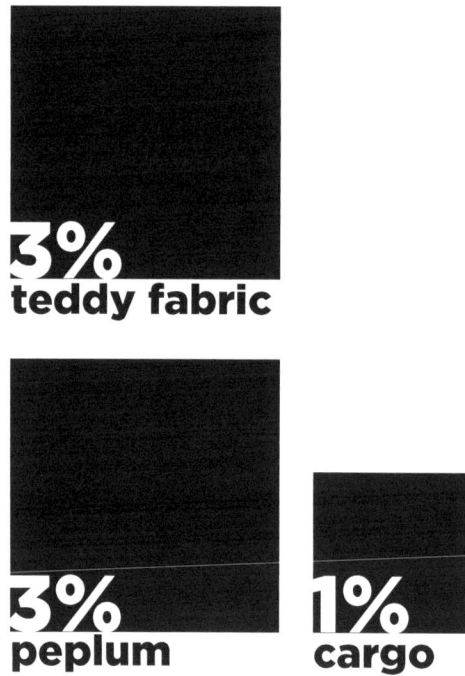

THE MICRO TRENDS*

*trends which were seen in less than 5% of Brandon Maxwell's runways this year

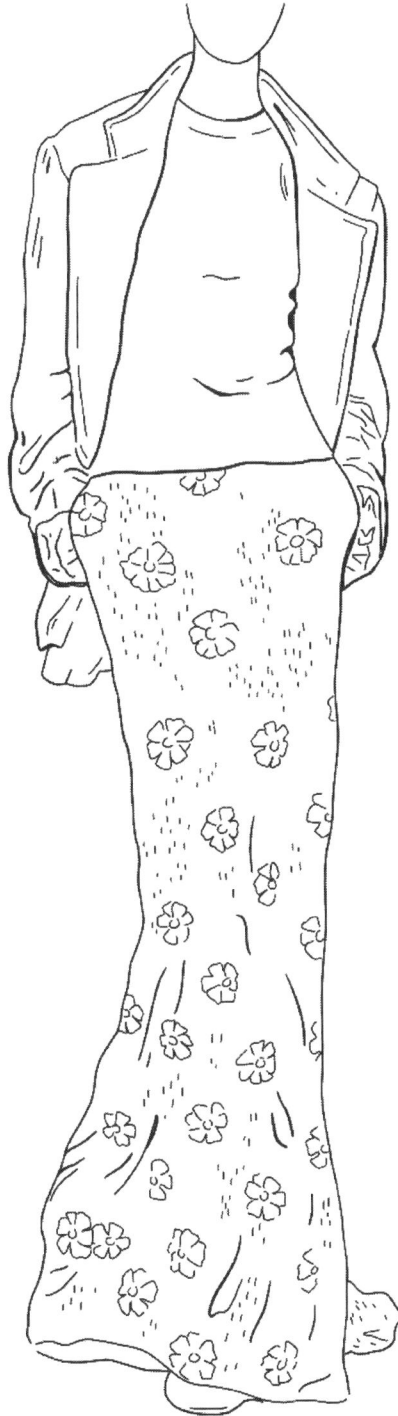

LOOK 34
SPRING / SUMMER 2023 RUNWAY

THE FABRICS

26%
shimmer

26%
patterns

4%
sheer

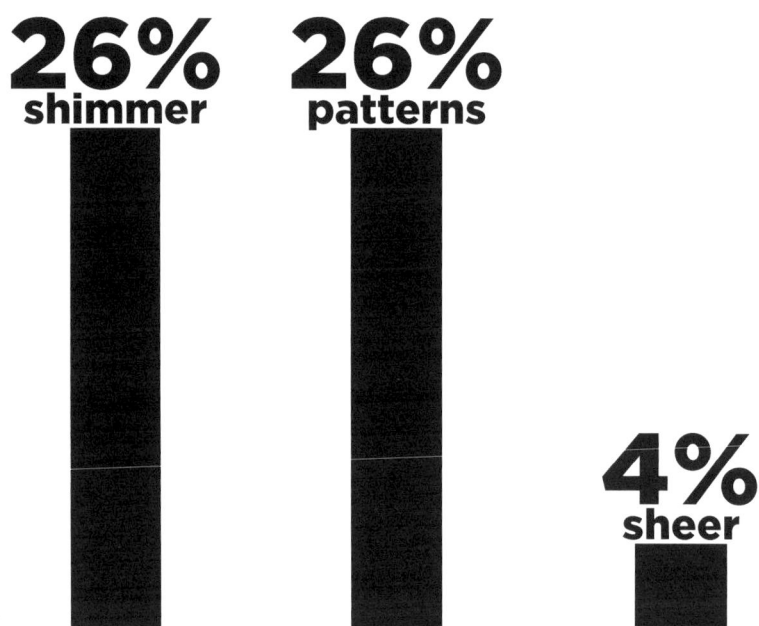

woven throughout Brandon Maxwell's collections were an assortment of fabrics — from floral printed gowns and pants, to shimmering mini dresses, to long, sheer layers

LEATHER, FOR FALL

leather was seen in tailored blazers, maxi-length dresses and skirts, jackets, and cropped-tops in Brandon Maxwell's Fall collection — an over 150% increase from the Spring runway

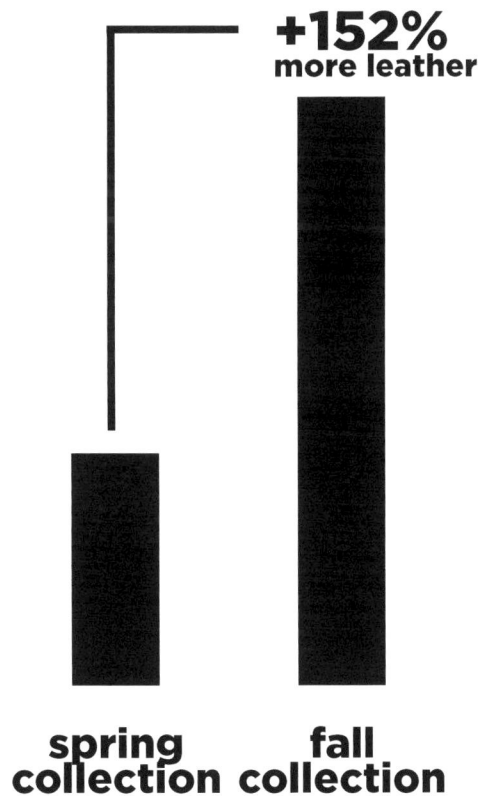

+152%
more leather

spring
collection

fall
collection

CHANEL

designed by Virginie Viard

CLASSIC CHANEL

30% logo

66% costume jewelry

costume jewelry was consistently the biggest trend across Chanel's collections this year — a style of chunky, prominent jewelry Coco Chanel is credited for pioneering

THE BAGGAGE

Chanel's iconic handbags were seen throughout its runway looks this year — following another ~15% increase in price for its Classic Handbag

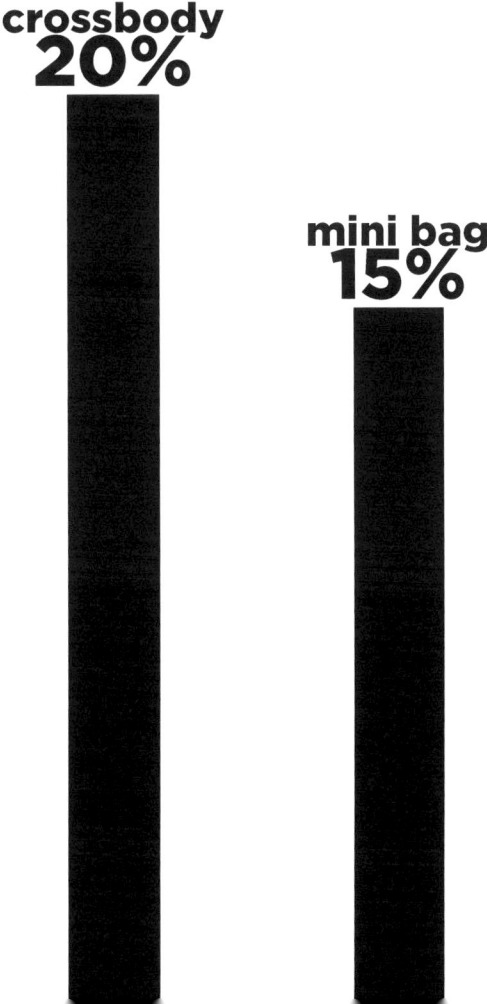

crossbody
20%

mini bag
15%

18%
shimmer

10%
tweed

7%
feathers

4%
lace

SHINING IN TWEED

Chanel's signature tweed looks sparkled on the runway — literally — with tweed, shimmering skirts, dresses, and blazers dominating the fabric lineup

MORE COVERAGE, PLEASE

accents across Chanel's collections offered opportunities for additional coverage, from high necklines to leg-warming fashion

tights, 26%

knee-high socks, 9%

turtleneck, 3%

-90%
monochrome

**spring
collection**

**fall
collection**

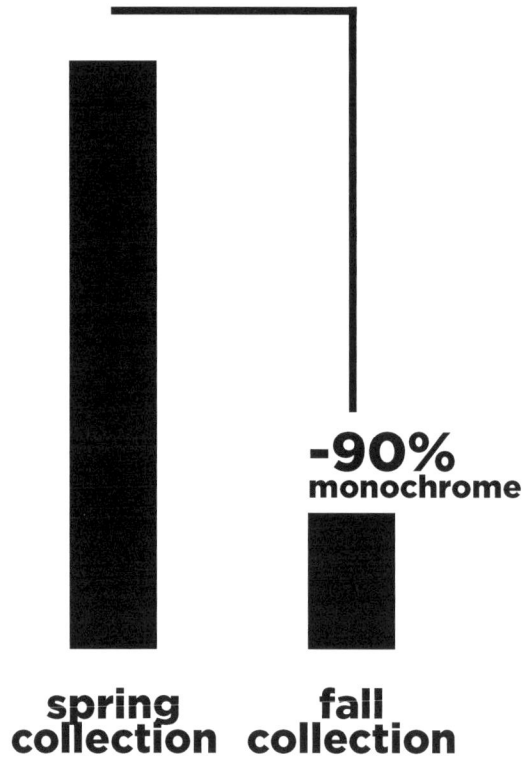

MOVING AWAY FROM MONOCHROME

the mainly monochromatic looks from Chanel's Spring collection were replaced with colorful patterns and pops of color on the Fall runway

50%
patterns

11%
3-dimensional
embroidery

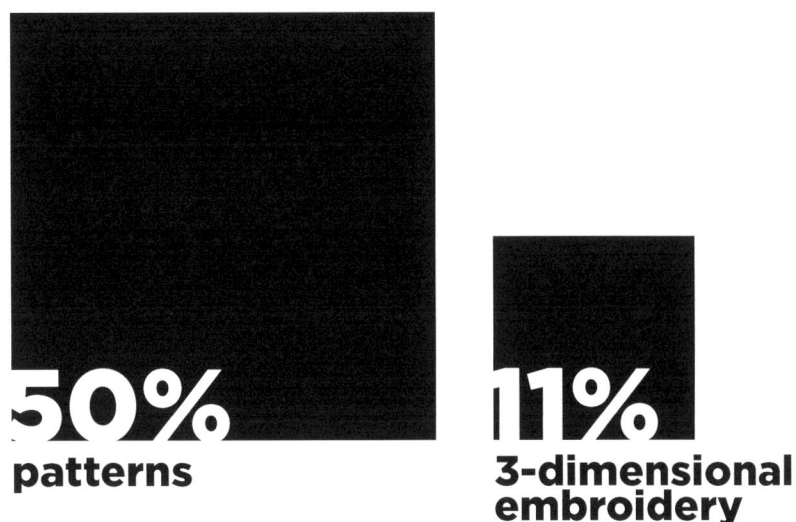

TRANSFORMING PATTERNS

3-dimensional embroidery refers to when the polka dots on a sweater are made of fabric roses, or when floral patterns are decorated with feathers poking out of the fabric — as seen on Chanel's Fall runway

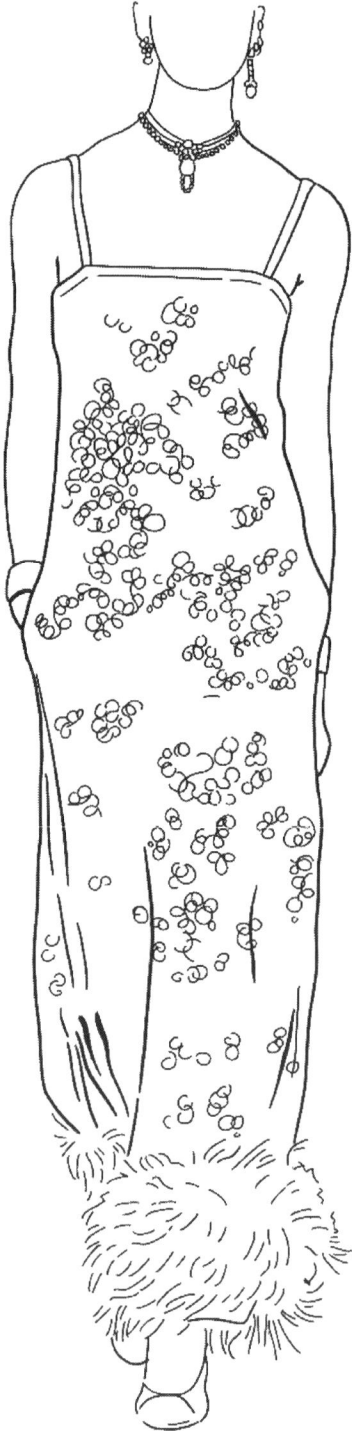

LOOK 55
SPRING / SUMMER 2023 RUNWAY

LESS (LENGTH) IS MORE

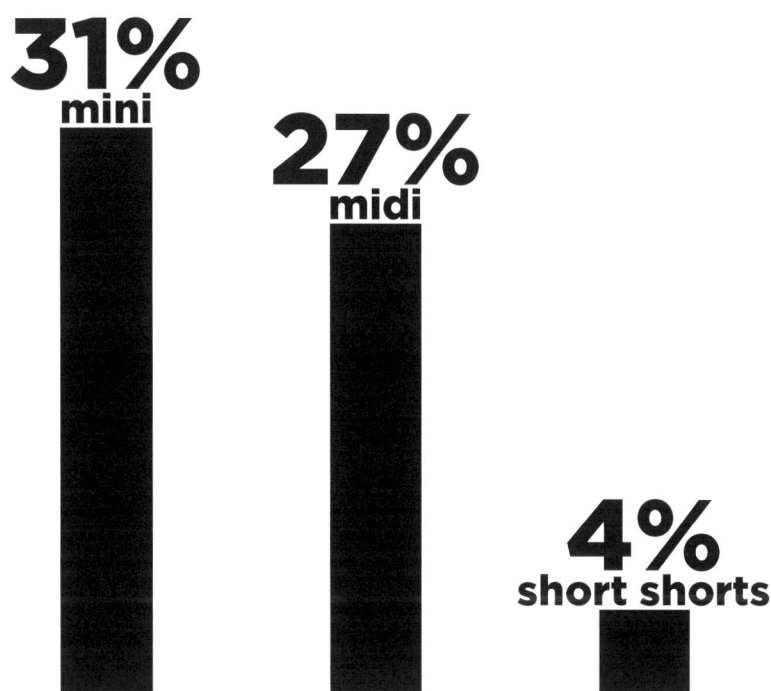

31%
mini

27%
midi

4%
short shorts

many of the looks on Chanel's runways this year exhibited short, mini-length hemlines, which were far more popular than full-length pants, or below-the-knee hemlines

DIOR

designed by Maria Grazia Chiuri

DIOR'S "NEW LOOK"

trends in Dior's collections this year payed homage to Christian Dior's signature "new look" — debuted in 1947, the silhouette included midi-length dresses and skirts with an accentuated waist

37%

dresses

66%

midi-length

64%
knee-high socks

23%
headbands

20%
gloves

THE ACCESSORIES

from sheer, knee-high socks in the Spring
collection to leather gloves and padded
headbands in the Fall, Dior's collections this
year were full of accessories

STAYING WARM

from long, plaid or leather coats to
teddy-lined bomber jackets, Dior offered
several variations of outerwear in this year's
collections

long coat
13%

bomber jacket
7%

LOOK 16
SPRING / SUMMER 2023 RUNWAY

EXPOSED

trends from Dior's collection showcased different ways to expose some skin — from ultra-short shorts in the Spring collection to cleavage-baring necklines in the Fall

11%
plunging
necklines

10%
short shorts

10%
mini hemlines

MOVING AWAY FROM JEWELRY

Dior reduced the quantity of prominent, chunky jewelry accents by over 1/3 from its Spring to Fall runway collection

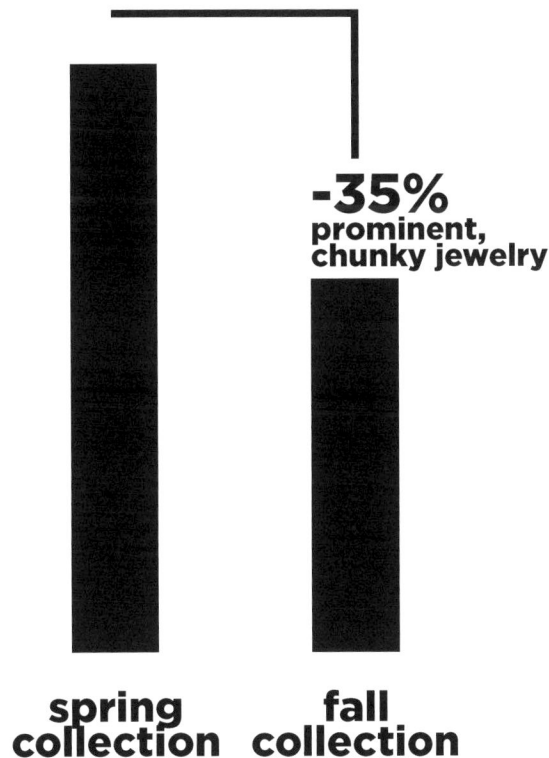

-35%
prominent,
chunky jewelry

spring collection   **fall collection**

I FEEL PRETTY

Dior's Spring collection included an abundance of lace — from sheer bralettes to lace-lined skirts and shorts — with delicate, floral embroidery throughout

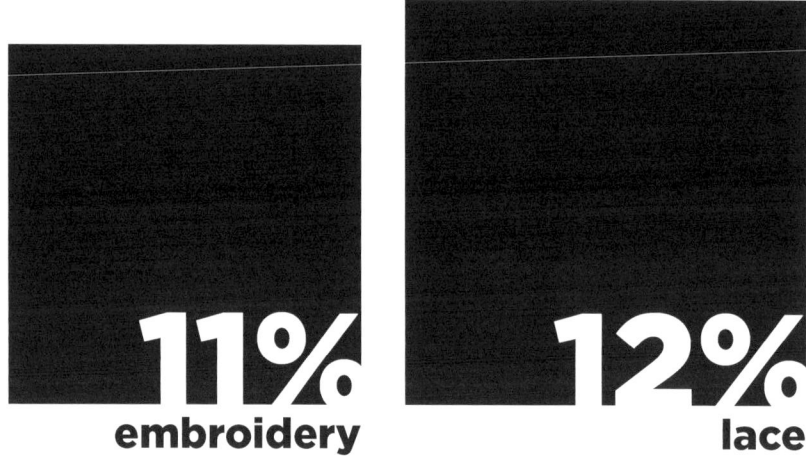

11%
embroidery

12%
lace

THE MICRO TRENDS*

*trends which were seen in less than 5% of Dior's runways this year

large zippers, 2% ████████████████████

tote bags, 2% ███████████████████

cargo fabric, 1% ██████

FENDI

designed by Kim Jones & Silvia Venturini Fendi

neon

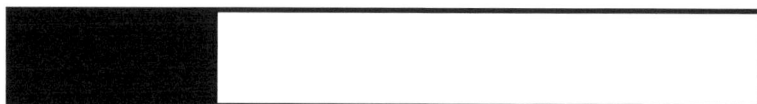

26%

SO BRIGHT

Fendi's runway collections had neon accents woven throughout — from neon
green bags and shoes in the Spring, to
neon pink dresses and pants on the Fall
runway

YOU CAN'T SPELL BAG WITHOUT "BAGUETTE"

Fendi's hallmark "baguette" shoulder bag, which celebrated its 25th anniversary this year, was the most popular bag seen on Fendi's runways

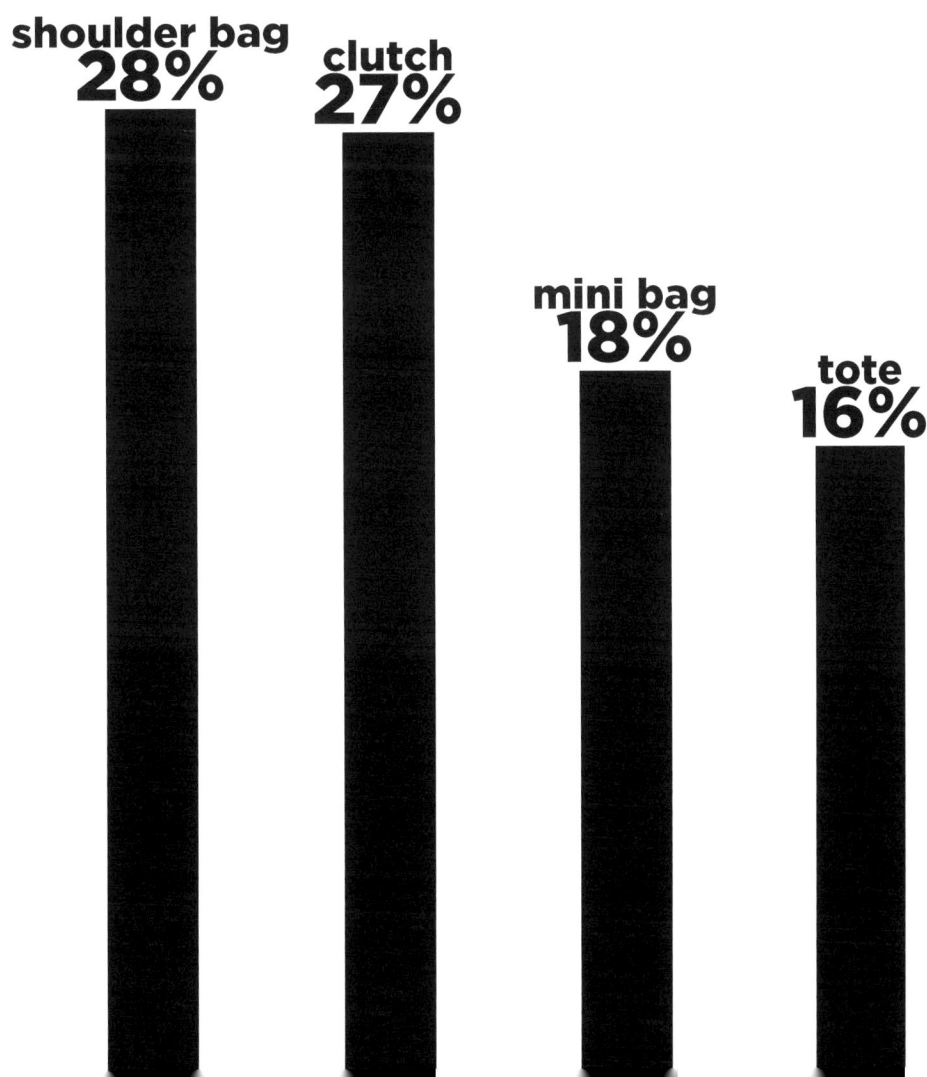

shoulder bag
28%

clutch
27%

mini bag
18%

tote
16%

CUT IT OUT

Fendi played with its fabrics this year, from dresses and skirts with slits running up the side in the Spring collection, to long, turtle-neck dresses with cutouts in the Fall

13%

slits

15%

fabric cutouts

logos
42%

SAY MY NAME

just under half of Fendi's looks this season
boasted the brand's iconic name and logos

LOOK 44
SPRING / SUMMER 2023 RUNWAY

MIDI IS KING

from sheer neon dresses in Fendi's Spring collection, to pleated skirts and collared dresses in the Fall, midi was Fendi's most popular hemline this year

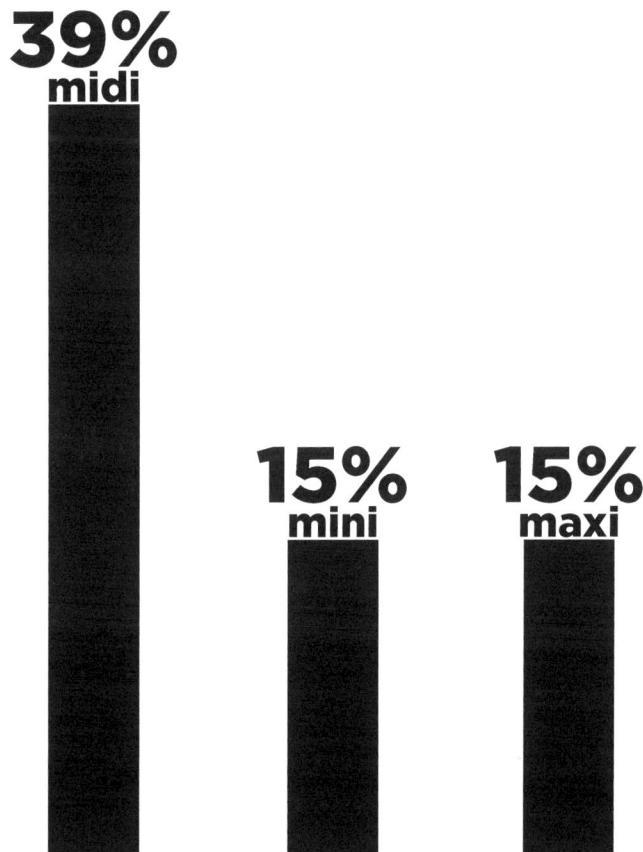

39%
midi

15%
mini

15%
maxi

MIDRIFFS FOR SPRING

Fendi's Spring runway collection included several looks with cleverly placed cutouts, or buttons left unbuttoned, to expose the midriff area — a trend seen far less in the Fall

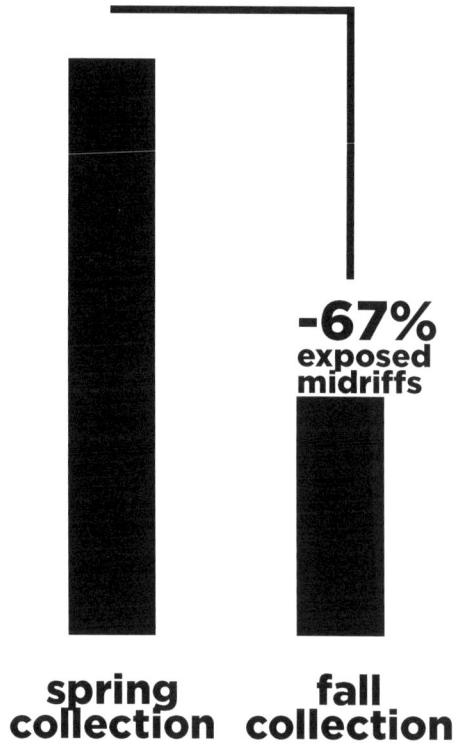

-67%
exposed
midriffs

spring
collection

fall
collection

NOT QUITE VEGAN

although Fendi states leather and fur are at the "core" of the brand's heritage, Fendi shared a target of achieving a "comprehensive global certification and traceability system for natural fur that guarantees animal welfare and environmental standards" by 2023 for 100% of its fur

9%
leather

7%
fur

GUCCI

designed by Alessandro Michele

SUNGLASSES INDOORS?

the most popular trend tracked across Gucci's collections this year was sunglasses, seen in nearly half of the brand's runway looks

48%
sunglasses

HORSEBIT IS BACK

the most popular bag on Gucci's Fall run-way — a re-edition of Gucci's 2003, Tom Ford-era large, horsebit clutch bag — was seen in in ~55% of the collection

shoulder bag, 35%

crossbody, 19%

clutch, 11%

THE ACCESSORIES

from neck scarves and ties under button-down shirt collars in the Spring collection, to dangling pearl earrings and feathered hats in the Fall, Gucci is never one to shy away from a bold accessory

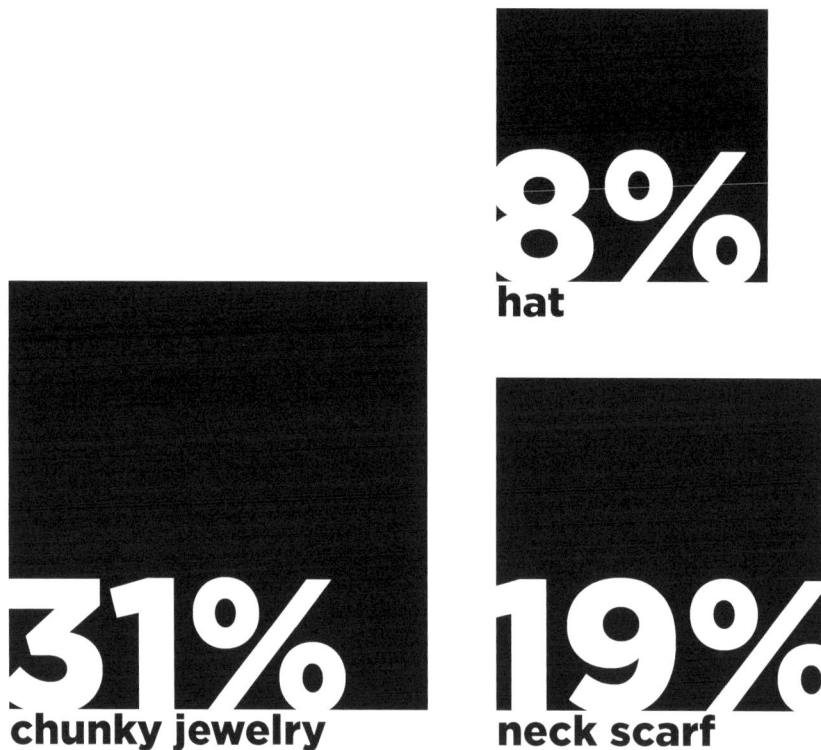

8%
hat

31%
chunky jewelry

19%
neck scarf

LOOK 14
SPRING / SUMMER 2023 RUNWAY

LOTS TO BARE

trends throughout Gucci's runways this year which exposed some skin — from crop-tops paired with low-rise pants in the Spring collection, to sheer, sleeveless dresses in the Fall

14% sleeveless

13% exposed midriff

12% slit

10%
fur

10%
snakeskin

8%
leather

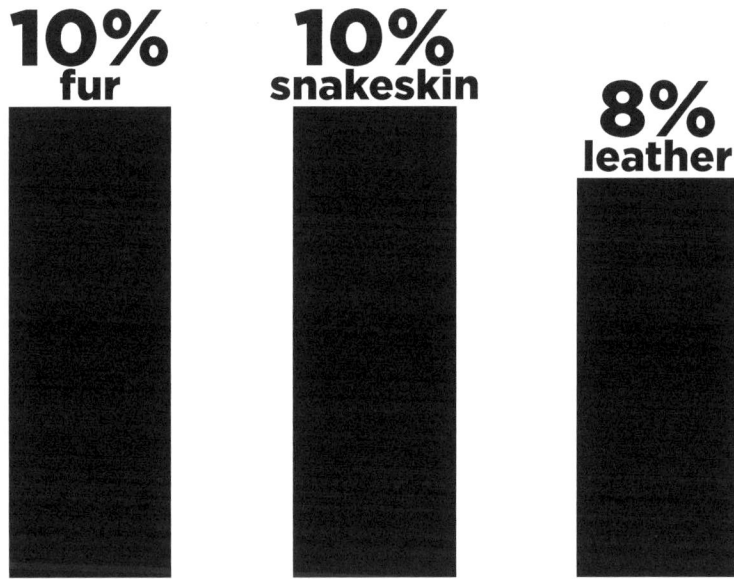

LIONS AND TIGERS AND SNAKES, OH MY

animal prints, fabrics, and hides were used
consistently throughout Gucci's collections
this year

LIFE IS GUCCI

Gucci's iconic name and double-G logo
were seen in nearly one-fifth of its runway
looks this year

logo

21%

THE MICRO TRENDS*

*trends which were seen in less than 5% of Gucci's runways this year

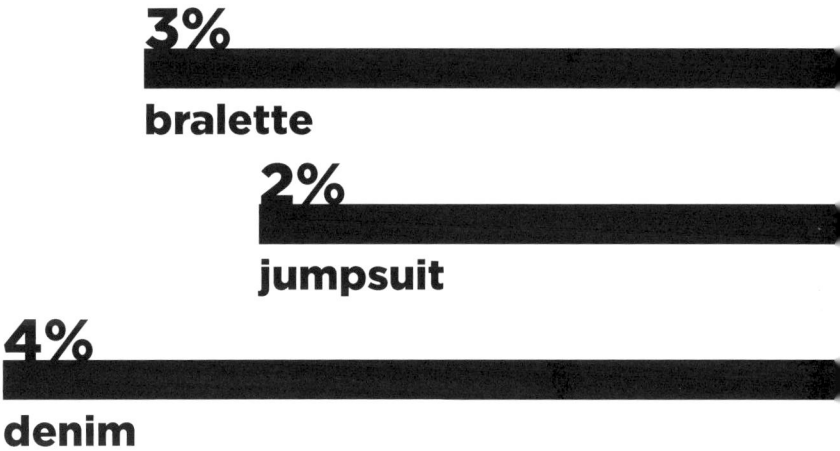

3%
bralette

2%
jumpsuit

4%
denim

HERMÈS

designed by Nadège Vanhee-Cybulski

AN HOMAGE TO HERMÈS

trends throughout Hermès' runway collections which paid homage to the brand's roots as a leather horse harness and equestrian accessories workshop, in late 1830s Paris

knee-high boots
28%

long coats
24%

leather
20%

knit, 7%

shimmer, 16%

FEELS LIKE...

knit tops and dresses were seen throughout Hermès' Spring collection, while shimmer-ing fabrics closed the Fall runway

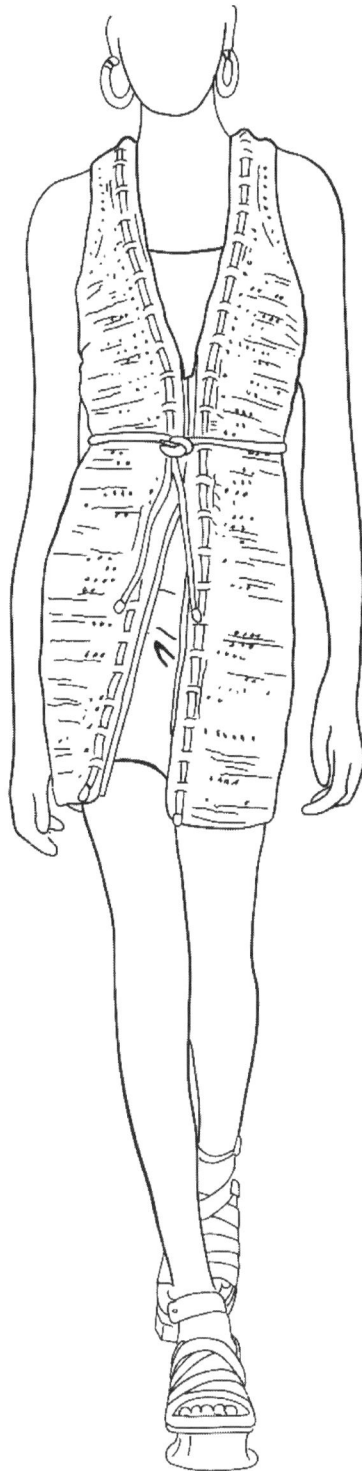

LOOK 16
SPRING / SUMMER 2023 RUNWAY

THE MICRO TRENDS*

*trends which were seen in less than 5% of Hermès' runways this year

2%
stripes

2%
cargo fabric

3%
off-the-shoulder tops

15%
turtleneck

11%
plunging

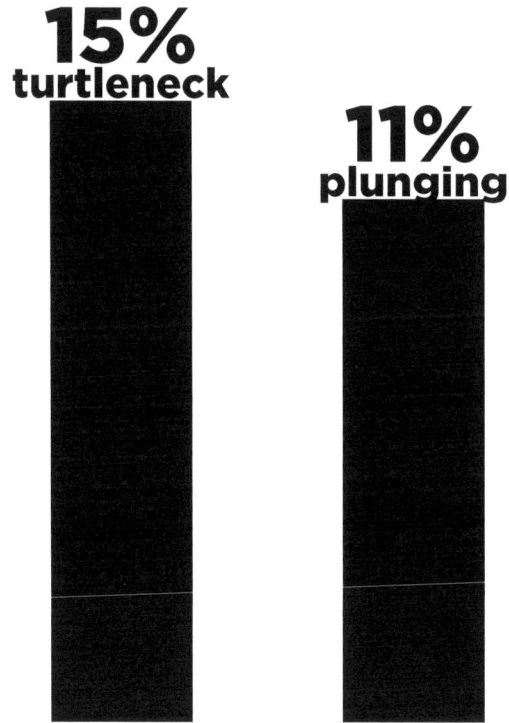

THE NECKLINES

Vanhee-Cybulski played with necklines throughout Hermès collections this year, from low-cut dresses and jumpsuits in the Spring collection, to turtleneck sweaters and dresses in the Fall

DRESSING UP

the most popular silhouette tracked across Hermès' collections this year was dresses, seen over four times more often than pants

42% dresses

10% pants

LOEWE

designed by Jonathan Anderson

LIFE IN 3-DIMENSIONS

3-dimensional accents were the highlight of Loewe's Spring runway, with large, plastic anthurium flowers placed on the breast of dresses and toes of shoes (see page 107)

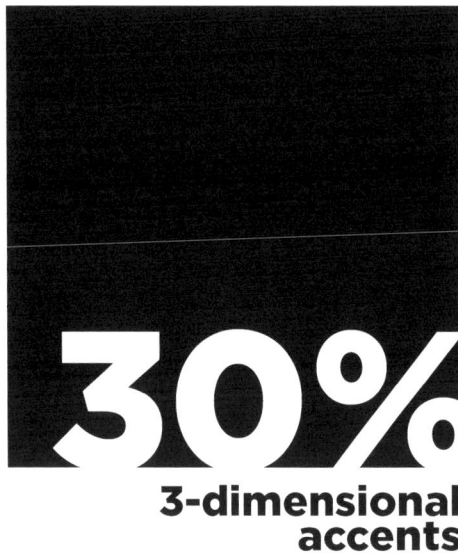

30%
3-dimensional accents

midi, 34% ████████████████████

mini, 23% ███████████████

maxi, 7% █████████

THE YEAR OF MIDI

the majority of Loewe's hemlines were midi
or mini — from ultra-short striped dresses
in the Spring collection, to midi-length satin
dresses over-printed with blurry patterns in
the Fall

CLOGGED

Loewe's runways this year re-introduced clogs into the high-fashion sphere, as the shoes were seen in 26% of the Spring looks and 12% of the Fall collection

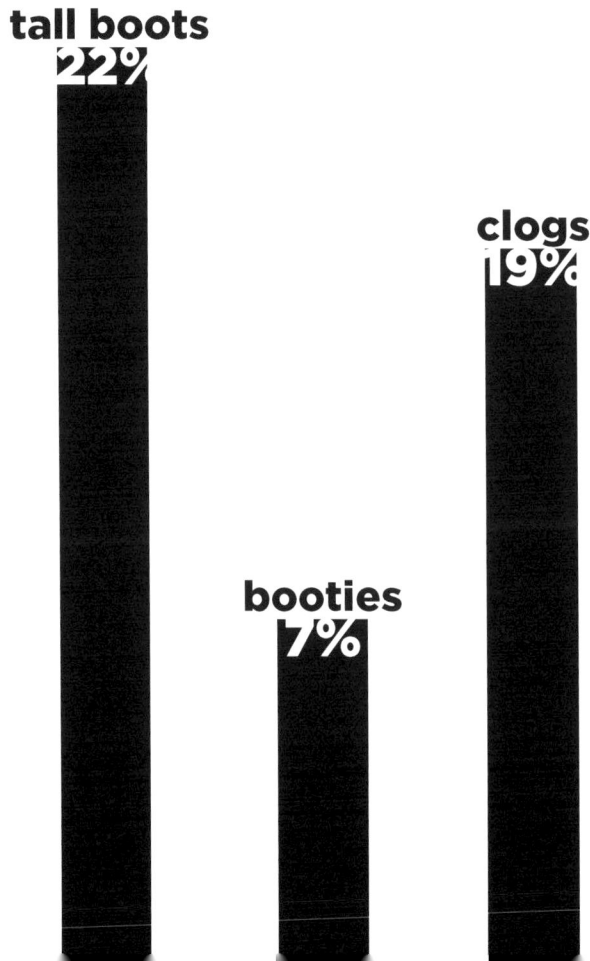

tall boots
22%

clogs
19%

booties
7%

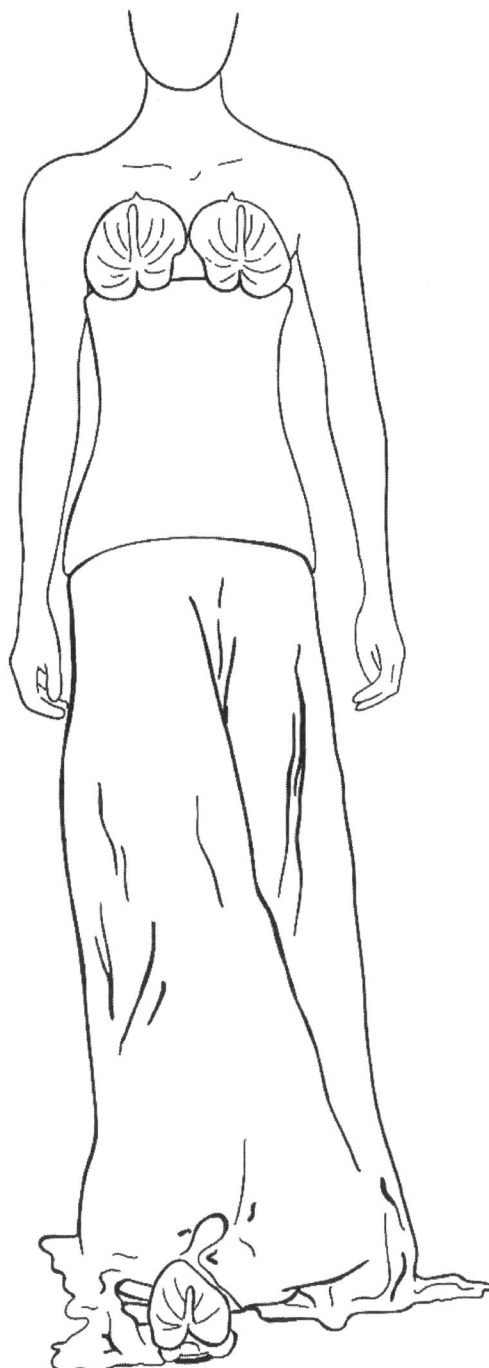

LOOK 35
SPRING / SUMMER 2023 RUNWAY

-23%
less maxi hemlines

spring
collection

fall
collection

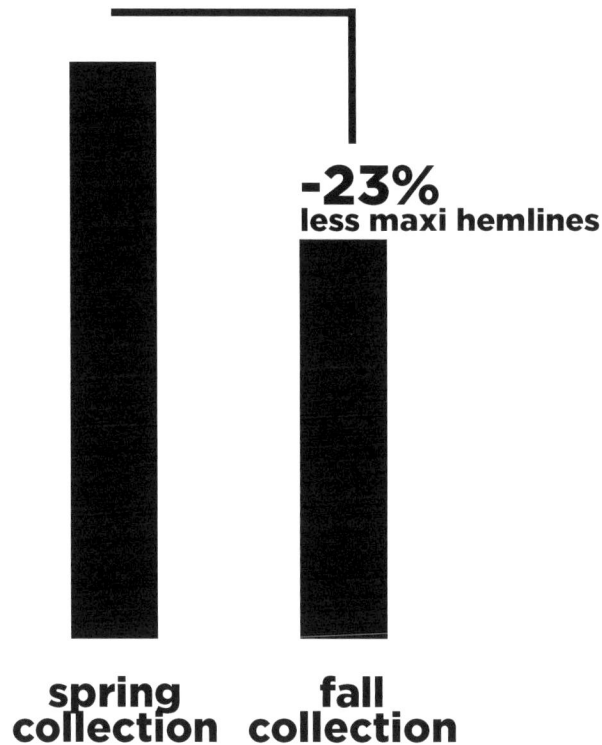

MAXI FOR SPRING

interestingly, the few (7%) of looks across
Loewe's collections with maxi-length hemlines were seen predominantly in the Spring
collection, as the Fall saw a 23% decrease
in the longer, warmer hemline

THE BAGGAGE

Anderson presented a variety of baggage options across Loewe's collection this year, from the brand's iconic "puzzle" shoulder bag, to woven leather pouches, to comical-ly large, monochromatic totes

27%
shoulder bag

11%
tote

LOUIS VUITTON

designed by Nicolas Ghesquière

LIVE LAUGH LV

Louis Vuitton's hallmark logos were only seen in 10% of its runway looks this year — 30% less than the industry average

COVER UPS

to stay warm, Ghesquière proposed long,
leather coats with oversized buttons in the
Spring collection, and patterned blazers
and bomber jackets in the Fall

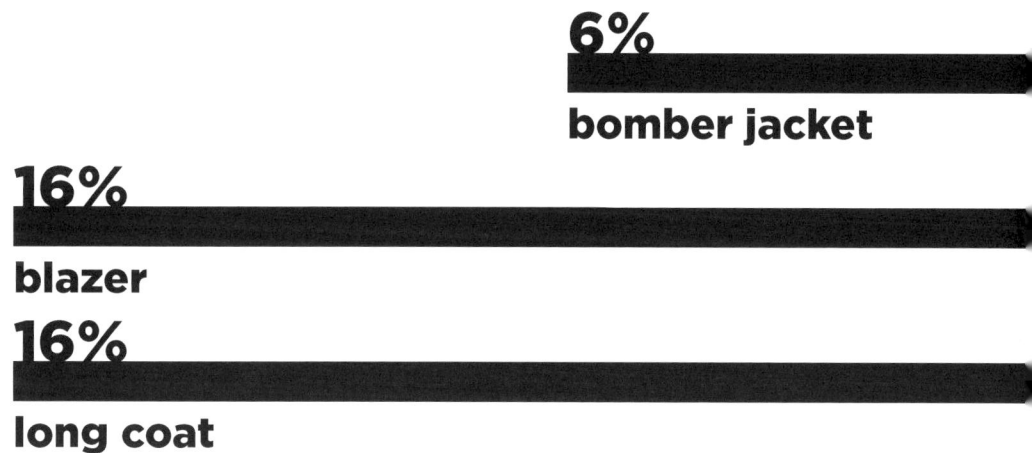

6%
bomber jacket

16%
blazer

16%
long coat

THE FABRICS

leather was seen in just under half of the brand's looks this year, from sleeveless mini dresses, to lining and pockets, to long, trench coats

leather
42%

shimmer
19%

lace
4%

THE FRENCH ACCENTS

Louis Vuitton's runways this year did not shy away from bold, innovative accents, including large, prominent zippers in jackets and mini dresses, thick belts covering the whole waist, and logo scarves tied around the neck

neck scarves, 8%

big belts, 23%

zippers, 22%

LOOK 46
SPRING / SUMMER 2023 RUNWAY

THE MINI-ER THE BETTER

one third of Louis Vuitton's looks this year bared mini-length hemlines — from short, leather dresses in the Spring collection to lace mini-skirts in the Fall

30%
pants

33%
mini

MIU MIU

designed by Miuccia Prada

LEGS LEGS LEGS

tights, 23%

knee-high socks, 22%

accompanying Miu Miu's iconic, ultra-short hemlines were several options for leg coverage — from knee-high socks paired with loafers in the Spring, to colored tights in the Fall

SO MUCH MIU MIU

logo

60%

Miu Miu's iconic logo was seen in the majority of runway looks this year — whether embroidered on turtleneck sweaters, embossed on leather handbags, or printed on the tongue of a sneaker

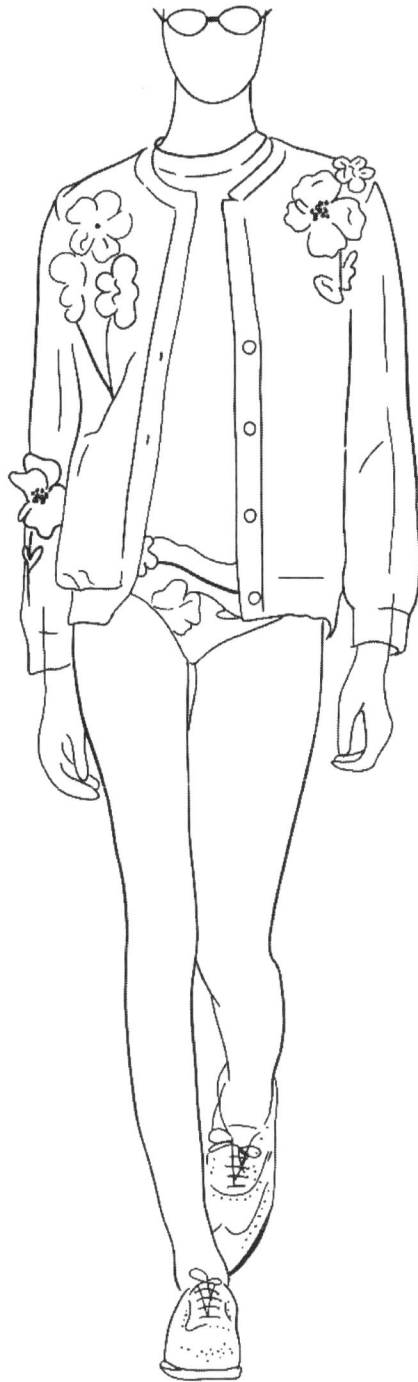

LOOK 39
FALL / WINTER 2023 RUNWAY

MINI MIU MIU

Miu Miu's hallmark short-hemline looks were seen throughout its runways this year — from ultra-short shorts in the Spring collection, to embroidered bikini-cut looks in the Fall

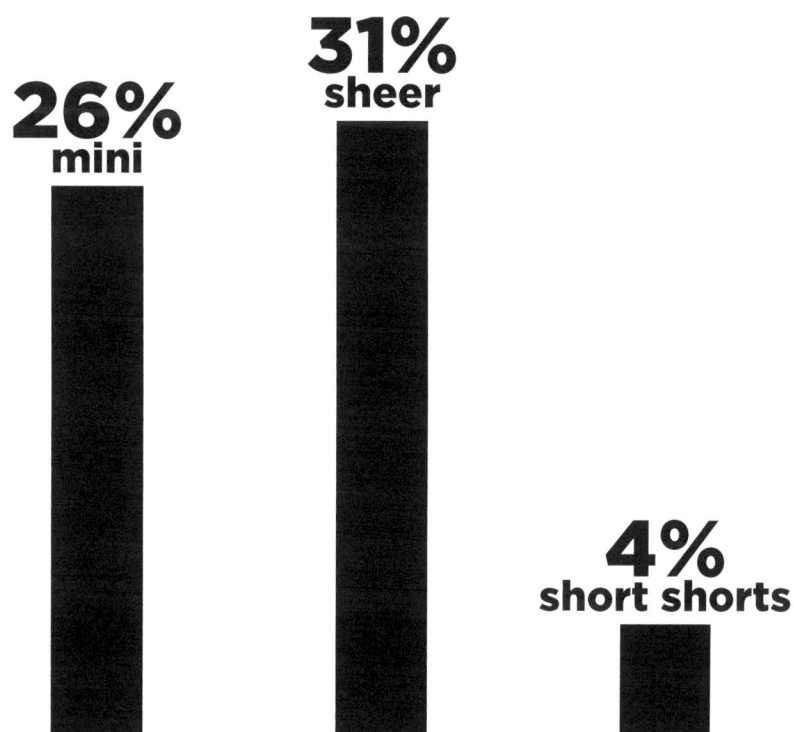

26%
mini

31%
sheer

4%
short shorts

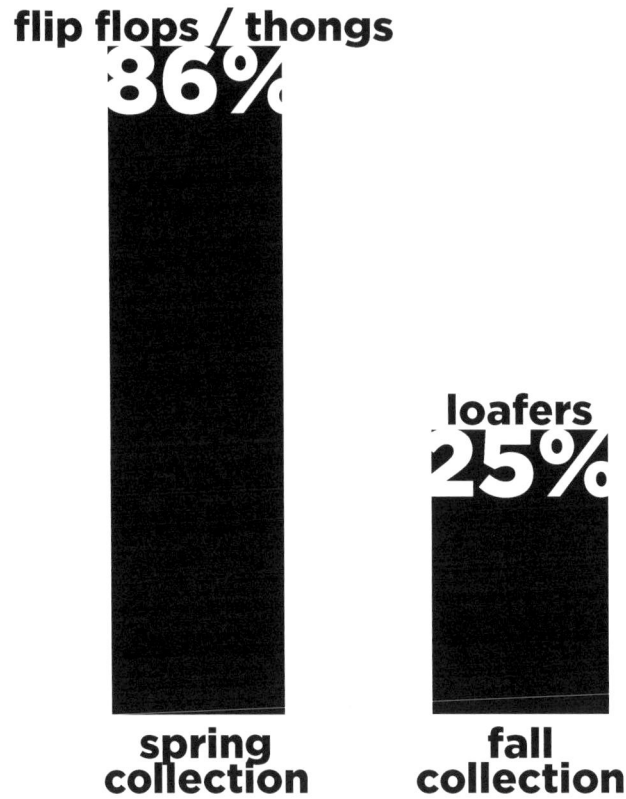

flip flops / thongs
86%

loafers
25%

spring
collection

fall
collection

THE SHOES

Miu Miu's Spring runway highlighted open-toed sandals and kitten heels, while the Fall collection showed off black and brown leather loafers

THE FABRICS

from leather bombers and hooded jackets,
to floral embriodery on sheer, midi dresses,
to distressed denim pants and blazers

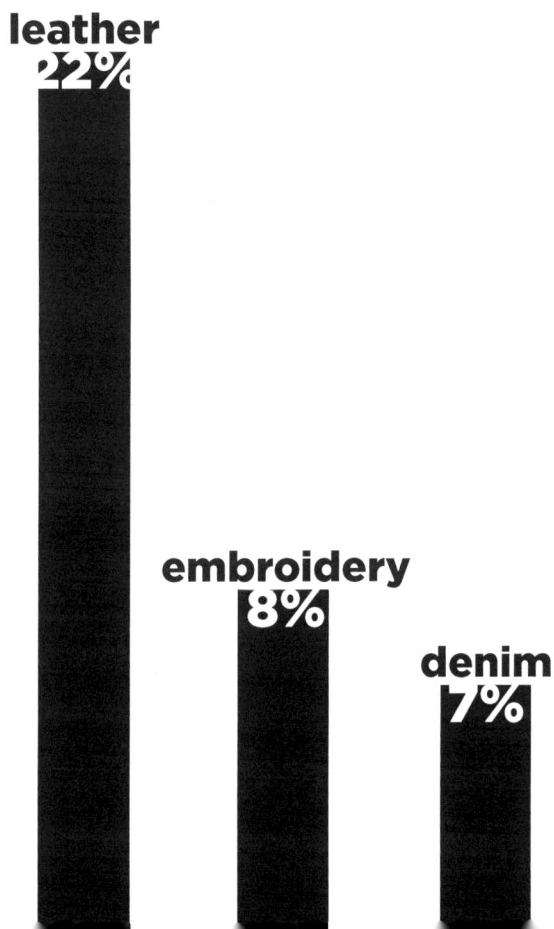

leather
22%

embroidery
8%

denim
7%

SAINT LAURENT

designed by Anthony Vaccarello

ALL ABOUT THE ACCESSORIES

the vast majority of Saint Laurent's models strutted down the runway with sunglasses paired with large, gold earrings and bangles

67%
chunky jewelry

81%
sunglasses

LOOK 25
SPRING / SUMMER 2023 RUNWAY

THE MICRO TRENDS*

*trends which were seen in less than 5% of Saint Laurent's runways this year

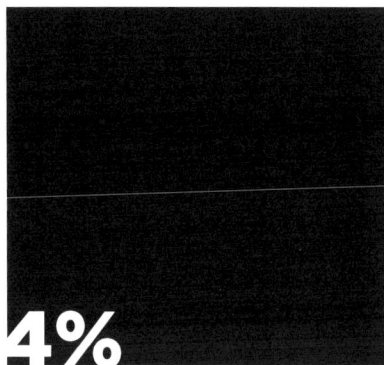

4%
t-shirts

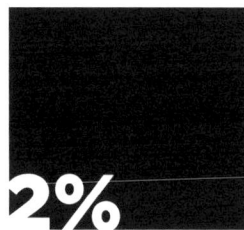

2%
one-shoulder tops

2%
pussy bows

open toe, 23%

pointed toe, 60%

THE SHOES

pointed toe pumps were seen in the majority of Saint Laurent's runway looks — whether patent leather or covered in colorful fabric

THE SAINT LAURENT SIL-HOUETTES

hooded dresses and tops were the high-light of Saint Laurent's Spring collection — and even featured on the cover of British Vogue a couple of months later — while long, sheer capes stunned on the Fall runway

hoods 23%

capes 18%

-94%
less maxi hemlines

**spring
collection**

**fall
collection**

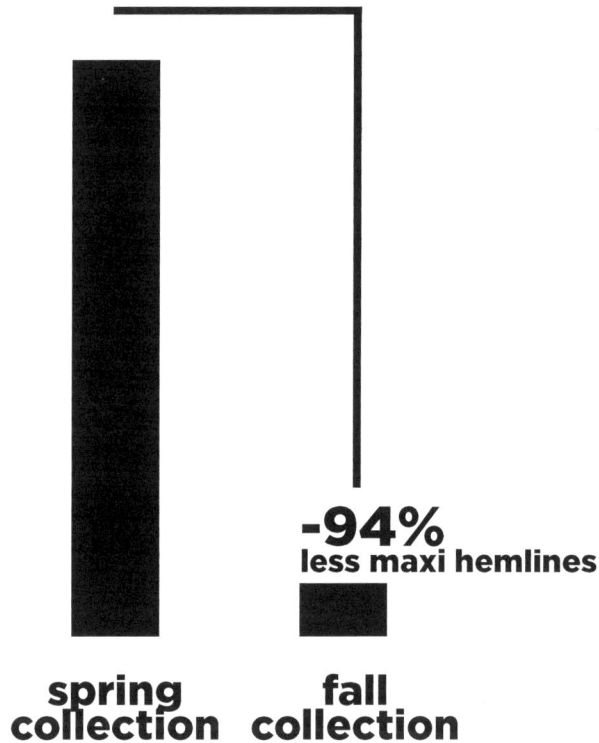

HEMLINES ARE GETTING SHORTER

maxi-length dresses and skirts dominated
Saint Laurent's Spring runway, while the
Fall collection saw an almost full reduction
in the longer, warmer hemline

VALENTINO

designed by Pierpaolo Piccioli

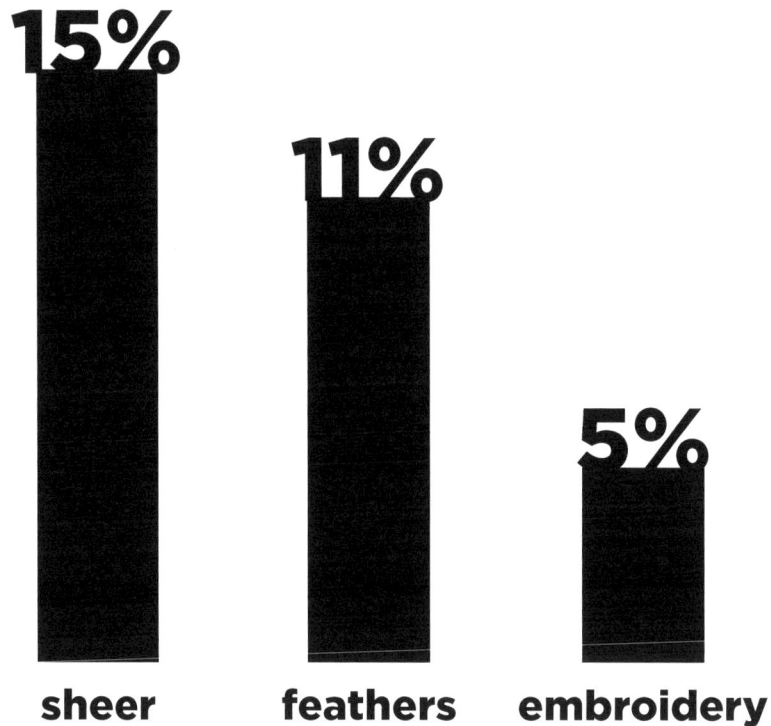

15%

11%

5%

sheer   **feathers**   **embroidery**

FEELS LIKE...

Valentino played with a variety of fabrics and textures this year, from feathers poking out of pants and dresses in the Spring collection, to sheer tops with floral embroidery in the Fall

SO MANY SHOES

Valentino's collections this year were lined with laced-up loafers, patent leather boo-ties, and the brand's hallmark studded, pointed-toe heels

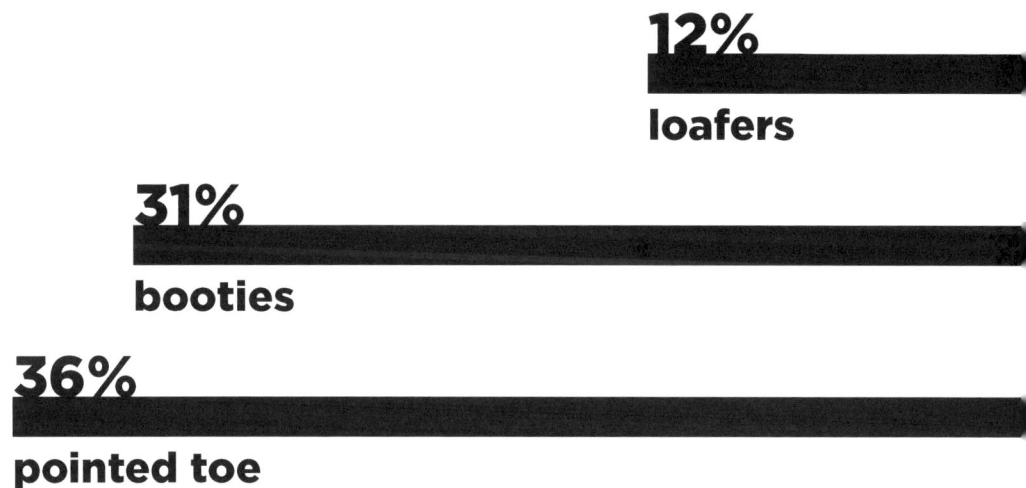

12%
loafers

31%
booties

36%
pointed toe

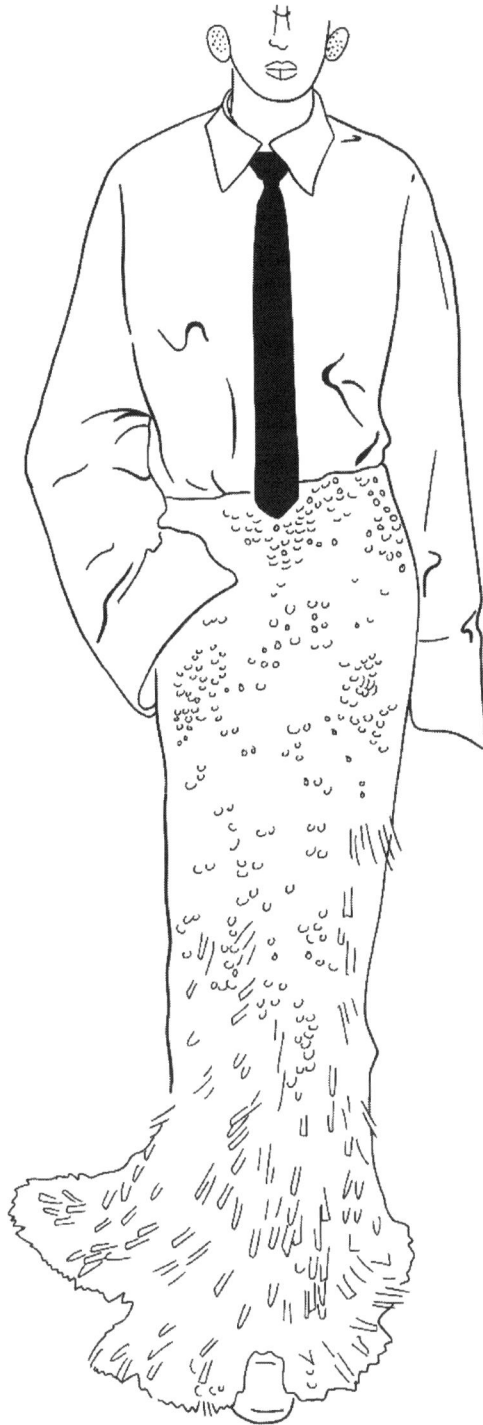

LOOK 73
FALL / WINTER 2023 RUNWAY

VERY VALENTINO

Piccioli, notoriously unafraid of playing with new, grand silhouettes, incorporated ball-gowns with long, flowing capes, and dress-es with exaggerated sleeves into Valenti-no's collections this year

capes
10%

big sleeves
6%

SHORT & LONG

ultra-short shorts and full-length pants were seen in equal proportions across Valentino's runway looks this year

12% short shorts

12% long pants

clutch, 33%

shoulder bag, 18%

tote, 7%

CLUTCHING ONTO VALENTINO

clutch bags were the most popular hand-bag at Valentino this year, followed by lo-go-covered shoulder bags and large, leath-er totes

VERSACE

designed by Donatella Versace

ALL COVERED UP...

Versace's Fall, star-studded runway was dominated by leather and colorful, fabric gloves, often worn with a pair of matching, colorful sheer tights...

40% gloves

27% tights

sheer, 20%

exposed midriff, 16%

plunging neckline, 12%

...WELL, NOT SO MUCH

...while the Spring runway was filled with looks daring to leave more skin exposed

LEATHER & LACE

leather and lace were seen together
throughout Versace's runways — from lace
bodices with leather straps to sheer, lace
dresses worn under leather coats

leather
48%

lace
10%

LOOK 50
SPRING / SUMMER 2023 RUNWAY

VERSACE VERSACE VERSACE

the brand's iconic name and head-of-Medu-sa logo were seen on bags, belts, and shoes

logo

23%

7%
buttons

9%
cutouts

THE ITALIAN ACCENTS

Versace knows how to make a statement
with her clothing, from making patterns
with fabric cutouts in the Spring collection,
to large, sparkling buttons on coats in the
Fall

MADE BY MADÉ

madé is a software engineer based in new york city, and the founder of "data, but make it fashion". her roots are in spain & cuba.

Made in the USA
Monee, IL
09 October 2023